Celebrating
ONTARIO

Celebrating
ONTARIO

JACK CHIANG

Fitzhenry & Whiteside

Copyright © 2004 by Jack Chiang

Published in Canada by Fitzhenry & Whiteside,
195 Allstate Parkway, Markham, Ontario L3R 4T8

Published in the United States by Fitzhenry & Whiteside,
121 Harvard Avenue, Suite 2, Allston, Massachusetts 02134

www.fitzhenry.ca   godwit@fitzhenry.ca

10 9 8 7 6 5 4 3 2 1

Library and Archives Canada Cataloguing in Publication

Chiang, Jack
        Celebrating Ontario / Jack Chiang.

Includes index.
ISBN 1-55041-341-4 (Ontario cover).—ISBN 1-55041-343-0
(Kingston, Ont. cover)

        1. Ontario—Pictorial works. I. Title.

FC3062.C44 2004   971.3'05'0222
C2004-903860-5

U.S. Publisher Cataloging-in-Publication Data
(Library of Congress Standards)

Chiang, Jack.
        Celebrating Ontario / Jack Chiang.—1st ed.
[192] p. : col. photos. ;   cm.
Includes index.
Summary: A photographic journey through the province of Ontario.
ISBN 1-55041-341-4 (Ontario cover)
ISBN 1-55041-343-0 (Kingston, Ont. cover)
1. Ontario – Pictorial works. 2. Ontario – Guidebooks. I. Title.
917.13/04/4   F1057.7.C535 2004

Fitzhenry & Whiteside acknowledges with thanks the Canada
Council for the Arts, the Government of Canada through the Book
Publishing Industry Development Program (BPIDP), and the Ontario
Arts Council for their support of our publishing program.

Cover and text design by Tania Craan

Printed in Canada

TABLE OF CONTENTS

To my wife Cathy and our children Christopher and Jeffrey Chiang;

Alastair, Adrian and Leslie Coleman.

Introduction

Asked to describe the province in which they live, Ontarians turn quickly to superlatives. It is Canada's most populous province with 12 million inhabitants, they will tell you. At 1,068,580 square kilometres, it is larger than many countries — twice the size of France, in fact. The provincial capital, Toronto, is the country's busiest commercial and financial centre. Niagara Falls is Canada's number-one tourist attraction. The CN Tower is the world's tallest freestanding structure. Yet beyond the bustle of its city streets, the province is rich in ways beyond the measurement of commerce, and any attempt at cataloguing that richness must always run the risk of omission. Mention the Niagara Escarpment, designated by the United Nations as an International Biosphere Reserve, the crystal clear water and the shipwrecks at Fathom Five National Marine Park, the scenic regions of Muskoka, Grey/Bruce Huronia, or Lake Superior Park, and someone will point you to the 1,000 Islands where the St. Lawrence River meets the eastern shores of Lake Ontario, the 30,000 Islands of Georgian Bay, or the magic of a day at Point Pelee National Park. Dare to mention the quiet beauty of small town Paris, Gananoque, Perth, Picton or Port Hope and the boosters of more than 100 other picturesque, historical towns and villages will challenge your choices.

To celebrate Ontario is to also celebrate the ethnic and cultural diversity of the province as it in turn celebrates the traditions of the many peoples from around the world who live here. Treat yourself to a taste of Shakespeare at Stratford, or enjoy a day at Niagara-on-the-Lake during the annual Shaw Festival. Visit the Kitchener-Waterloo area where strong German roots have given birth to the largest Oktoberfest in North America or Toronto, where the rhythms and laughter of the Islands fill the streets each year for the Caribana Festival, or any of the other communities where people of diverse backgrounds gather to celebrate with dragon boat races, St. Patrick's Day parades, Scottish Highland games, Greek food festivals, and dozens of other special events. To celebrate Ontario is also to celebrate the seasons: Ottawa's spring Tulip Festival, the autumn colour tours and agricultural fairs throughout the province, the winter carnivals, skiing, skating on the Rideau Canal, as well as the riverfests, white water rafting, air shows, Canada Day celebrations on Parliament Hill, and the many heritage festivals of summer.

In the pages that follow, you will find many more reasons for our celebrations. You'll see spectacular pictures of our scenic wonders, bustling cities, friendly towns and quaint villages. Come celebrate with us.

Celebrating
EASTERN ONTARIO

The 92.2-metre Peace Tower is dedicated to the 66,650 Canadians who were killed in World War I.

LEFT PAGE: Peace Tower, Ottawa

ABOVE: Sparks Street, Ottawa

BELOW: Canada Day celebrations

LEFT: National Gallery of Canada

CENTRE: This eight-kilometre stretch of the Rideau Canal is one of the world's longest skating rinks.

RIGHT: Samuel de Champlain monument

Canada Day and the War Memorial

Canada Day fireworks

Hot-air Balloon Festival

Byward Market

Canadian Museum of Civilization

The Parliament buildings, originally built between 1859-66, are among the most photographed edifices in Canada

Sparks Street in Ottawa

Town Hall, Carleton Place

Pembroke

White-water rafting

Historical re-enactment in Upper Canada Village

Upper Canada Village

ABOVE: Cornwall's Nativity Church

RIGHT: Seaway International Bridge in Cornwall

BELOW: Prescott

Highway 2 near Cardinal

The Thousand Islands region stretches from Brockville to Kingston, a distance of about 75 kilometres.

Depending on the water level, the Thousand Islands region has about 1,150 islands and islets.

ABOVE: Gananoque is known as the Gateway to the Thousand Islands.

RIGHT: The Village of Westport

BELOW: Perth, founded in 1816 as a military settlement, has a population of 6,000 people.

RIGHT PAGE: Downtown Kingston

NEXT PAGE: Downtown Kingston and its harbour

LEFT PAGE: Fort Henry

ABOVE LEFT: Fort Henry Guard

ABOVE RIGHT: Cathcart Tower in Kingston

British Prime Minister Winston Churchill once called retired Commodore Len Birchall "The Saviour of Ceylon."

Ray Ban Gold aerobatic-flying team on display.

Waupoos Island at Prince Edward Bay

Heidi Koven and her daughters Ainsley, 6,
and Jessica 3, celebrate Hanukah

Upper Canada Village

Frontenac Provincial Park north of Sydenham

Rideau Canal, which connects Ottawa to Kingston, is 198 kilometres long, and has 45 sets of locks. It was constructed between 1827 and 1832

Madoc

Marmora

The white Trillium is the official flower of Ontario

RIGHT PAGE: Tamworth, north of Napanee

Float Your Fanny Down the Ganny river race along the Ganaraska River in Port Hope.

Cobourg was founded by the United Empire Loyalists in 1798.

Lindsay

Prince Edward County

RIGHT: Downtown Peterborough

RIGHT: Peterborough's Lift Lock

ABOVE: Trenton is located at the mouth of the Trent River.

LEFT: United Empire Loyalists first settled in Belleville in 1784.

Celebrating
THE GREATER TORONTO AREA

Toronto Downtown

LEFT: Old buildings co-exist with new ones in Toronto's downtown.

ABOVE: The Toronto Islands Park provides a good view of downtown Toronto, including the SkyDome and the CN Tower.

About 350,000 people go to see the Royal Agricultural Winter Fair and Royal Horse Show each November.

An estimated one million people watch Toronto's Santa Claus Parade.

Toronto's famous Caribana parade

ABOVE: Edwards Gardens

BELOW: Casa Loma, built by Sir Henry Pellatt in 1911-14, has 98 rooms.
It is open to the public and self-guiding tours are available

RIGHT: Scarborough Bluffs

Sharon Temple in Sharon

Slovak Catholic Cathedral of the Transfiguration

H. H. Goode & Son feed and farm store in Uxbridge

The Beaches of Toronto

The CNE is Canada's largest fair

Dragon boat races, Toronto Islands

Toronto Chinatown

Rodeos are popular throughout Ontario

A view from the Toronto Islands.

Downtown Toronto, viewed from the Sky Pod at the top of the 1,815-foot CN Tower.

Ontario Place is an amusement park that features canals, lakes, lagoons, rides, a miniature golf course and a cinesphere.

Major highways connect Toronto to other parts of Ontario.

A giant mural depicts Oshawa's industrial heritage. Oshawa's nickname is The City in Motion.

Oshawa's war memorial

ABOVE: Toronto's City Hall was designed by Finnish architect Viljo Revell.

LEFT: Nathan Phillips Square

Toronto waterfront

ABOVE: Queen's Park

LEFT: Toronto waterfront

Celebrating
SOUTH-WESTERN ONTARIO

Hamilton

The American Falls is higher but narrower than the Canadian Falls.

Niagara Falls is Canada's best-known and most photographed tourist attraction. About 12 million people see it each year from the Canadian side.

Niagara's Skylon Tower

ABOVE LEFT: Niagara-on-the-Lake, home of the Shaw Festival

ABOVE RIGHT: Historic preservation is an important part of Niagara-on-the-Lake
and the restored 1864 Prince of Wales Hotel is an example.

Fort Erie

Hundreds of the world's top cyclists competed in Hamilton for the world championships.

The Royal Botanical Gardens, located between Hamilton and Burlington, has 1,100 hectares of flowers, gardens and 30 kilometres of walking trails.

Hamilton is an industrial centre known for its steel production. Its harbour is one of the largest on the Great Lakes.

Port Dalhousie

Webster's Falls near Hamilton is one of the most spectacular
and accessible waterfalls along the Niagara Escarpment.

Balls Falls in St. Catharines.

Guelph Armoury

Guelph's Church of Our Lady Immaculate

Early morning near Waterloo

Cambridge

St. Catharines

Port Dalhousie

The annual Niagara Wine Festival parade in St. Catharines.

Royal Henley Regatta in St. Catharines

Harry Peterson uses his head during the Oktoberfest in Kitchener-Waterloo.

LEFT: A Mennonite family in St. Jacobs

ABOVE: The University of Western Ontario

RIGHT: Downtown London

Chatham's First Presbyterian Church.

Stratford City Hall

War memorial in Brantford

Farming is a big industry in Western Ontario.

The Welland Canal was first opened in 1829.

Welland

The Ambassador Bridge, which connects Windsor and Detroit, is
one of the busiest points between the United States and Canada.

Odette Sculpture Park in Windsor

Sarnia is a busy centre for marine traffic.

Wallaceburg is well-decorated for Christmas.

LEFT: A heron patiently waits for its next meal in Stratford

ABOVE: Swan on the Avon River in Stratford

RIGHT: A heron in Windsor

Point Pelee, mainland Canada's southernmost point, is a popular place for birdwatchers and naturalists.

St. Thomas is famous for its life-size statue of Jumbo the Elephant,
which was killed by a train in 1885.

LEFT: The Mohawk Chapel in Brantford, is the oldest Protestant church in Ontario and the world's first Royal Native chapel.

CENTER: Major-General Isaac Brock's statue at Queenston Heights.

RIGHT: Grand Bend is a popular resort town on Lake Huron.

Celebrating
CENTRAL ONTARIO

Algonquin Provincial Park

Algonquin Provincial Park is 7,725 square kilometres of wilderness.

ABOVE: Dorset

BELOW: Bruce Trail

RIGHT: Dwight

Bala

Wasaga Beach, 14 kilometres long, is one of the longest freshwater beaches in the world.

Collingwood

R. M. S. *Segwun*, built in 1887, is one of the oldest steamships in North America

Ron Baird's Spirit Catcher in Barrie

Midland

Near Whitefish Falls

A competitor waits for his turn during a pow wow on Manitoulin Island

LEFT PAGE: The Goderich town "square" is an octagon.

LEFT: Bruce Peninsula

ABOVE: Parry Sound

BELOW: Orillia

PREVIOUS PAGES: Tobermory is famous for its sunken ships and the Flowerpots.

Wiarton Willie is one of the world's most famous weather forecasters.

LEFT: Bruce Trail stretches from Tobermory to Queenston Heights, 780 kilometres away.

ABOVE: Fergus

Port Carling

153

Celebrating
NORTHERN ONTARIO

Lake Superior Park

Old Woman Bay

Batchawana Bay is located between Sault Ste. Marie and Lake Superior Park.

North Bay is strategically located in the Blue Sky Region. The Dionne Quints Museum honours five of North Bay's most famous residents.

A rainbow appears south of Kirkland Lake, a town that produced
more than 40 million ounces of gold in the 20th century.

LEFT PAGE & ABOVE: Moose Factory is an island on the Moose River at James Bay.

ABOVE RIGHT: Moosonee, the Gateway to the Arctic, is inaccessible by road.

Science North, a hands-on science centre, is Northern Ontario's most popular tourist attraction.

Sudbury

Sudbury's famous nine-metre-high Big Nickel

Ramsey Lake

Onaping Falls

Sturgeon Falls

Sault Ste. Marie

Sault Ste. Marie's waterfront

Lake Superior Park covers 1,565 square kilometres.

Lake Superior Park

More than 85,000 people visit the Agawa Canyon each year.

Eagle Canyon and its 100-metre suspension bridge.

Mining has been an important part of Bruce Mines (BELOW LEFT), Kirkland Lake (ABOVE LEFT), and Timmins (RIGHT)

The 41-metre Kakabeka Falls near Thunder Bay is known as the Niagara of the North.

Terry Fox's larger-than-life statue.

The Sleeping Giant near Thunder Bay is a geological formation that resembles a person

ABOVE & LEFT: Old Fort William in Thunder Bay was a 19th-century fur-trade headquarters of the North West Company

LEFT PAGE: Timmins is known for its silver-zinc and gold mines

Batchawana Bay

Crocker Lake

Wawa's famous giant goose

Photo Introduction

Modern cameras are so automatic that almost anybody can take properly-exposed pictures. However, there are a few things that you have to know in order to take better pictures:

1. SHUTTER DELAY

All cameras have a shutter delay. When you press the shutter button, the camera does not take a picture right away. It has to focus its lens, calculate the correct exposure and, if it is too dark, decide whether its flash should be activated. All these actions take time. This delay is one of the most frustrating things for beginners. However, you can reduce this shutter lag. Most cameras have a two-stage release system. You can reduce this delay by pressing the shutter button half-way down. By doing so, you lock the focus and the exposure. Then, if you press the button all the way, you can take the picture almost instantly.

2. CAMERA SHAKE

Many photos entered in any contest are eliminated because they are not sharp. It is difficult to hold a small camera steady. Many digital cameras have so many buttons on them that there isn't much room left for your hand. One of the most useful accessories you can buy is a tripod. If you don't have one, you can still take sharp pictures. Just use whatever support you can find. Place your camera on any solid object: a book, a shelf, a mail box or a coffee mug.

3. CENTRE OF INTEREST

A good picture should have a centre of interest, and it doesn't have to be placed right in the middle of the picture. The centre of interest is your message, the reason why you take the picture. What are you trying to say in this photo? It should be obvious to any viewer what this message is.

4. DE-CLUTTER

Most amateur pictures do not have a clear message because they are too cluttered. You can eliminate those distractions by moving closer to your subject, moving to one side or zooming in. A famous war photographer once said: "If your photos are not good enough, you're not close enough. That applies to other photographic situations, too.

5. BE PATIENT

Don't take any picture just because you're ready. Take it when your subject is ready. If you want a picture of your Aunt Annie, wait until she has a good expression, or when she is doing something interesting. If you want a picture of your children swimming, wait until you can see their faces, or when they have a good expression. If you want a picture of the exterior of your cottage, wait until the lighting is good. Landscape photographers often have to wait for hours for the right light. Many of them visit and re-visit a site dozens of times before they can capture exactly what they want. Many of the pictures in this book were done that way — after many visits to the same location.

The following examples should further help you take better pictures.

Page 136

Sometimes a good picture just waits for you to take it. I was driving on a country road near Baysville, in the Muskoka area, when I saw these odd couples minding their own business — the geese were waddling behind the horses. I got out of my car just in time. If I had been a couple of seconds late, the geese would have wandered too far away from the horses. I used a Canon EOS-1RS film camera with a long lens for this picture.

Page 148-149

My son Christopher and I were on a cruise like this one at Tobermory one day when our boat went over one of the sunken ships in the area. I realized then that I should have been up in a plane. When we got back on shore, I tried to charter a local plane but none was available. The next day, I got my pilot friend Keith Watson to fly me from Kingston to the Bruce Peninsula — three hours away. We got there just in time for several pictures with my Canon 1D digital camera and a telephoto lens.

Page 36-37

I got this picture by chance. I was working late one spring evening. When I drove by the Kingston Harbour on my way home, I glanced back and saw this incredible sunset scene. I happened to have the right camera — a medium-format Hasselblad — with me. I took 10 pictures of this scene before it became too dark. Half a dozen of those pictures were ruined during processing. Fortunately, one good frame survived.

Page 10

Most amateurs like to take pictures like this but do not know how. It is easy. With a manual camera, just set the shutter speed to T or B for 10 to 20 seconds. Set the aperture at about f/8. Use a shorter exposure time if you are close to the fireworks and there are lots of shells exploding in the sky. Most point-and-shoot cameras also have a night-scene setting that allow you to take shots like this.

Page 43

Luck often plays an important role in photography and this picture is a good example. I was off work one day because I had to paint the window frames of my house. When I happened to look outside, I saw a small snake on a tree at my front door. I grabbed the camera, a Canon D30, and quietly went outside. I could not believe what had happened: A damselfly had landed on the head of the snake! After I took a couple of pictures, I went inside to get my Hasselblad camera for a better-quality shot. When I went back outside, both snake and damselfly were gone. I don't know what happened to the dragonfly.

Page 73

The best night-time shots are not taken at night. They are taken at dusk — within half an hour after sunset. You can consult the web site: www.sunrisesunset.com for the sunset time in your area. I knew the sunset time for Toronto before I went up to the top of the CN Tower for this shot.

Page 60-61

It is difficult to photograph buildings well. Most cameras makes buildings look like they are about to fall over. To photograph buildings well, you need an old-fashioned view camera, or a 35-mm camera with a perspective-control lens — to keep the lines of the buildings parallel. This picture was taken with an ARCA Swiss 6x9 FC camera that uses medium-format film. Most of the pictures of buildings and cityscapes in this book were taken with this camera.

Page 174

The Agawa Canyon north of Sault Ste. Marie is one of the most scenic spots in Ontario. I knew I needed a camera that would give me a larger slide for better quality. I also knew that I had to hike up many flights of stairs to the top of the canyon. I settled on a motorized Hasselblad camera with a wide-angle lens for this shot.

Page 162

Science North, in Sudbury, is one of Ontario's most popular tourist attractions. I had to go back to the same spot several times before the lake was calm enough to reflect the lights. Again, the best time to shoot night photos is just before it gets completely dark.

Page 92-93

When several hundred of the world's top cyclists competed in Hamilton, I knew I had to get a shot of them in a pack. I pored over the drawing of the race course and settled on a spot up the hill, just before they had to make a sharp turn. I used a Canon 1D digital camera with a 500mm lens.

Page 88-89

The Skylon Tower in Niagara Falls is probably the second most photographed landmark there — after the Falls itself. This picture presented itself when I walked toward the Horseshoe Falls early one evening. I had to go back two more evenings before I was successful because the strong winds blew the mist toward this particular site, drenching both me and my camera. The spotlights at left were used to illuminate the Canadian Falls while the ones at right light up the American Falls. The tools I used for this picture were an ARCA Swiss 6x9 FC view camera, a 55mm lens and an umbrella.

Page 118

Patience is a good thing to have if you want to take good pictures. I waited for this heron for three hours before it waded into the right spot. The first time I tried to get closer, the bird flew away. Then, a local resident told me that the heron lives in the area and if I waited long enough, it would come back. It did.

Index